Other works by Marty

Novels
The Assignment (Trevor and the Dark Rider series)

Bilingual Children's Books
A Spot On The Wall / Una Mancha En La Pared *(English, Spanish)*
Snail Parade / El Desfile de los Caracoles *(English, Spanish)*
Winston T. Mouse *(Chinese, Danish, English, German, Hebrew, Indonesian, Italian, Japanese, Korean, Nepali, Spanish)*

Motivational Materials
Believe. Do. and Follow Through!
A Stone's Throw *(parable)*
A Stone's Throw – Reflective Journal…To Improve Your Life
An Agreement with Life
To Touch the Infinite

How-To Books
Write A Children's Book (The Workbook): Impact the World
How To Help Others Become Successful

CYCLES / REAL ESTATE
Knowing The Future In Real Estate: Which Way It's Headed And How To Profit From It

Poetry Collections
Morning Coffee; Making Sense of It All; Letting In, Letting Out; 'Tis Worth; Gathering Light; Geese Will Fly

Calendar
I'm Just Sayin'

Songs
Raised Country, You're An Angel, There Would Be Roses, Place In Delhi, Ribbon Of Highway, Trust In Him, An Amazing Thing, What About, Wrestle, Things Of This World, My Trust, Up In Heaven, River Valley, Wings Of The Angels, Sweet Summer Sky, Tennessee Morning, JoAnn

(www.Amazon.com/author/reep)

Believe.

Do.

and

Follow Through!

by

Marty Reep and Isaiah Whittaker

©2011-2015 by Marty Reep & Isaiah Whittaker
All rights reserved. No part of this book may be reproduced, stored in a retrieval system or transmitted in any form or by any means without the prior written permission of the publishers, except by a reviewer who may quote brief passages in a review to be in a newspaper, magazine, journal, or website.

2015 edition.

Cover photo by Simon Reep.

ISBN-10: 0-9755820-6-2
ISBN-13: 978-09755820-6-0

To schedule Marty and Isaiah to speak to your group or organization, please contact them via:

mjreep@yahoo.com
home@whittz.com

Published by
Marty Reep
Lompoc, CA

To

My wife…for being a sounding board
and for keeping me focused all these years.
~ Marty

And

My parents…for all of your encouragement
and life lessons.
~ Isaiah

*Also, thanks to everyone who inspired stories in this book
and who helped make it become a reality.*

Contents

Believe. 9
    Believe that You Can!.. 10
    Get Rid of "Stinkin' Thinkin'" 14
    Developing Right Attitudes and Keeping Them. 16
    What's Your "Why"?.. 18
    Daily, Living Leadership 20
    Mental Magnetism 24
    Are You Where You Want to Be? 28
    From Hoping to Knowing 32
    Miracles, Luck, and Strokes of Genius 34

Do. 37
    Focus on Your End Goal....................................... 38
    Break Big Things into Smaller Pieces 41
    Seeds of Greatness 43
    Just Do It 46
    Doing, with Purpose... 48
    Living with Perceptions 50
    Do Something – Don't Just "Plan" 54
    Why? Because Your Life Counts! 56
    Enjoy What You Do... 58
    Living Through Expectations! 61

and Follow Through! 65
   Live Out Your Purpose in Life 66
   How to Handle Distractions................................ 70
   Tenacity... 74
   Choose to Live Differently 76
   Lean into the Wind... 78
   Overcome 80
   Realization of a Dream 84
   Handling Success and Recognition..................... 88
   Savor Life, One Moment at a Time 90

   My Goals... 92
   Epilogue 96

Section I:

Believe.

1

Believe that You Can!

"As a man thinks in his heart, so he is," – an idea written thousands of years ago, still holds true, today.

What you think about yourself and about others will determine your beliefs, your actions, your moral character, and your outcomes in life. It really will. Just look around you. The way that people live – where, how, and with whom – is determined by what they think about themselves and others.

If people think that they can succeed at something, they will. If they think they'll fail at something, they will. Either way, determinations are made with the thoughts they have.

What do you think about yourself?

Along with internal perceptions, each of us has a purpose in life and the potential to fully achieve it. How do you achieve your full potential in life? By believing, doing, and following through on some key things.

It all starts with the right mindset. If you have the right mindset, then the right beliefs and right actions will follow. If you have in your mind the ideas that will propel you into success, you are on your way to achieving your full potential.

Before you determine what it is that you need to do to become successful, you have to determine what it is that you want:

- What are you after?
- What is it that you want to do?
- What do you want to accomplish?
- How do you want to live?
- What kind of person do you want to turn into?
- What kind of legacy do you want to leave behind?
- Where do you want to live?
- Into whom do you want to invest time and energy?
- Do you see the way you are to go?
- Does your path seem clear?
- Who do you need to come alongside of you to give you input, encouragement, and direction?
- Who can you help as you're growing in your purpose and determination?

All those things matter, because ultimately, they will help shape you into the person you need to become.
When we wait to do something because we're afraid, we have just given in to the "screaming abdabs" (internal struggles) that mentally chase each of us. When you say, "No," to them and you no longer give them credence, then you have entered into the land of success and are walking on the road you were meant to traverse.

Most people stop short of their full potential by killing off the dreams they have with self-sabotaging thoughts. But, when you purposefully put forth in your mind the ideas that will propel you along a path of success, you are adding to your belief that you can succeed in what you do.

You may not succeed at first, but if you continue…you will succeed!

Believe that you can!

BELIEVE. DO. AND FOLLOW THROUGH!

NOTES:

2

Get Rid of "Stinkin' Thinkin'"

Do things from your past still hold you down? You don't have to let them do that anymore! Sometimes, people get stuck in ruts, and they don't even know it. They just keep getting up, doing the same thing – day after day – without so much as a second thought.

Ways you can mentally get rid of the past:

1. Write down what happened, and then burn the paper. …An amazing thing happens when you see those negative thoughts turn into ashes and go up in smoke!

2. Tell somebody else about it, and then tell yourself that what happened never has to happen again.

3. Envision a different past – one that you would have wanted to happen. …The subconscious mind is an incredible thing – you can dilute negative things with enough positive ones to heal damaged emotions, psyche, etc.

4. Wear a loose rubber band on your wrist. Whenever you start to tell yourself, "Yeah, but..." pull the rubber band, and let it snap you on the wrist. When it stings your wrist, tell yourself, "Yes, I can!" It'll only take a few times before your subconscious mind will correct itself. It may take more than a few times... it may take a few days. But, it'll be worth the change, in the long run.

NOTE: *This exercise is not meant for self-abuse! It's to be a brief correction for improving your attitudes in life.*

5. Lastly, move on! Stop telling yourself those things from the past that keep trying to hold you down or hold you back. Just "Press Delete."

Change your thinking.

NOTES:

_____

_____

_____

3

Developing Right Attitudes and Keeping Them

Whenever you go into a new situation, do you think, "They're out to get me," or "I bet everything's going to be great"? Whichever one is in the back of your mind will determine how you approach the situation and how you react to what happens in it.

Make sure that you have right attitudes about life in general, not just when starting something new.

Why?

Because...

1. You'll be happier.

2. You'll be less stressed.

3. Walking around smiling is more fun than frowning, right?

AND

4. You'll live longer and healthier!

Think about some of the people you've known or met during your life. Remember the people who seemed to be happy most of the time, no matter what? And, do you remember any grouchy people? Which of those two types inspired you? Maybe both did, but just in different ways.

If we model our lives after others who we want to be like while still being our unique selves, we will live successfully every hour of our lives. There's no way around it. Each of us can live out our personal best, if we'll remember to do so.

Right attitudes make a difference.

NOTES:

_____

_____

_____

_____

_____

4

What's Your "Why"?

***If you know the "why,"
you'll figure out the "how."***

That's a curious thought, isn't it? But, it's true. If you know "why" you're going to do something, then "how" to do it will fall into place, in due time.

That's just it, though - a lot of people don't know why they do things; why they're going to do things; or why anybody else does things. They don't have a real reason for reaching a goal – so, a lot of times, they don't.

However, when you give yourself a task to accomplish, your mind kicks into gear and tries to figure out ways to get it done. That's the subconscious mind at work – it doesn't distinguish fact from fiction – it just absorbs. On the other hand, your conscious mind has to have a valid reason to do something before it will support the energy necessary to achieve the goal.

So,
- What's your goal?
- What's your "Why"?
- What's the reason that you want to do it?
- What gets you out of bed in the mornings?
- What motivates you to work hard and to press onward when the going gets tough?
- Is it purely personal?
- Does it focus on others?
- Does it have greater depth than you realize?
- Will it carry you forward on its own waves of energy, long after the initial excitement has worn off?
- Is it something worth fighting for?

If it helps, write out your reason for wanting to do something. Then, think about it. Does what you wrote say what you thought it would? If not, think some more, and rewrite it.

When it does say what you mean, then read it aloud so that your own ears hear you say it. That way, both your subconscious and conscious minds can get to work.

Know your "why."

5

Daily, Living Leadership

People ask us, "How did you guys become so successful?" Our reply is usually something along the lines of, "Well, we came up with an idea, and we did it. We kept telling each other that we could do it, and we didn't listen to anybody who told us otherwise!" We took all of our other experiences in life and parlayed them into greater ones. From those came a myriad of ideas for books, videos, seminars, and other things to help people.

Once in a while, imagine what you would see if you could sit out in space and look at the whole world. Think about what you would want to change, if you could – and then start with yourself. We've done that very thing over the years, and it's worked!

In organizations and groups, some people look around at everyone else wishing that the others would "shape up," "change," "improve," or "be different." Instead, why don't YOU BECOME the kind of person you wish others would be? Then, by example, you can spur others on to greatness with your daily, living leadership. Will you do it perfectly? Never. But, shooting for greatness and failing will still land you and your colleagues/friends/family in a much better place than before. By combining your servant-heart with your leader-heart, you will learn to master servant-leadership on a daily basis as you do the things that you need to do.

Life doesn't happen all at once, thank goodness. It happens one day at a time. So, use that to your advantage – meaning, during your 24 hours today, positively work towards your dreams, goals, and ideas. Hopefully, you already do that and not just when you're reminded to, because some major thing happens in your life.

Part of the reason that major things happen to us is to jolt us awake from our sleepwalking through life. Some people forget to wake up (mentally) when they get out of bed in the morning. One of God's ways of reminding us to live to our fullest is to allow exciting, big, and sometimes scary things to happen to us. Those things jolt us enough, hopefully, to help us "get the lead out," and to get moving in the right direction, again.

Success breeds success, and greatness attracts greatness. When you launch out and do something inspirational, other like-minded people will contact you and want to be a part of what you're doing – not that they couldn't do things on their own, because they do – but because they know the amazing power of collaboration and combined force.

You may go through some hard times with people you collaborate with, but one of the greatest things that will come out of it is friendship. We all have a deep need for friendship – for positive relationships – and the more you invest your life in others, the deeper and richer the rewards will be for everyone around.

So, BELIEVE in what you're setting out to do. Live adventurously, and let your leadership shine to others. They need it as much as you do!

Live out leadership, every day.

BELIEVE. DO. AND FOLLOW THROUGH!

NOTES:

6

Mental Magnetism

How do you utilize the universal principle of attraction in your life? By thinking about and focusing on the best aspects of life and continuously dwelling on them. When you do that, a smile will appear on your face. Then, others will see it in your eyes, your smile, your attitude, and your overall demeanor.

Whether you realize it or not, every day, you promote and live out what you focus on. What you occupy and preoccupy your mind with is what you wind up seeing and being drawn towards.

If you focus on trouble and problems, you'll see and experience more trouble and problems. If you focus on successes and great things, you'll see and experience more successes and more great things. So, if what you're currently drawn to is what you really want in life, then good – way to go!

If not, then you can do something about it – change your thoughts! Change your focus! Adjust your position to something so that your perspective is different. When you get in the right position, all sorts of things become clear and in focus.

It's like using binoculars. When they're out of focus, you don't see things clearly. But, when you adjust the position or the focal point, everything becomes crystal clear! ...Amazing how that works. ...just like in life!

**Therefore, dwell on those things, ideas, emotions, and parts of life
that you <u>want</u>
and are interested in.**

Thinking about things is an automatic part of your daily existence – it's part of your overall build as a human being. But, you have control over the **content** that you think about. You attract or magnetize things to you, automatically – both good and bad.

Then, how do you attract only the good things? ...by focusing more of your thoughts, actions, reactions, and energy on them. As you do, the bad things will fall away, since less energy is being utilized towards them.

To better understand these concepts, think about magnets. Magnets work on the principles of attraction: North attracts South, South attracts North, over and over again, in a linear and circular series. It may seem that North and South are opposite, but in fact they are simply two different parts of energy that are intertwined throughout all aspects of life. One cannot exist without the other. They balance each other and hold each other up.

If you take those intertwined forces of energy and utilize them on emotional, physical, and psychological levels, amazing things will happen. When you deliberately and purposefully act and react with good intentions in all the different aspects of your life, you'll be amazed at the wonderful things that will happen – you'll start attracting the kind of people you want to you; things will start to seem "easy"; and "doors" will open that were closed before.

If you focus **internally** on the positive aspects of life, then **outwardly** conducting your life in the same way will be simple to do. In time, your life will change for the better.

Remember, you're not going for short term, overnight changes… you're working on things that will carry you through the rest of your life.

**What you focus on
is what you experience.**

7

Are You Where You Want to Be?

Wow! What a topic to think about! This *one* topic can cause so much inner turmoil inside of the average person. To truly answer the above question, you have to be really honest with yourself.

Have you reached a state of self-fulfillment, or are you just getting by from week-to-week, telling yourself, "things are going to get better"?

> Most people I know are living in the things-will-get-better state. I found myself there, once in my life, until I took a painful journey of dealing with reality.
>
> The first thing I had to do was identify my current state. I was not happy with myself or my marriage. As much as I wanted to fix my marriage and keep it together, my spouse did not...
>
> I had finally woken up from a 13-year fantasy to face reality. In addition to my marriage situation, I was not getting things in life accomplished the way I expected them to be accomplished. I was floundering in acceptance of my situations.

What happened next was a true miracle, in my eyes. My counselor, Julie Ramsey at the time, asked me a question that unlocked everything that was holding me back. It was like someone had lifted a 100-pound weight off my chest!

After 13 years of my current situation, I could finally see all aspects of my relationship. It was like I was totally naked to the truth. The sad part of this was I realized that I was living a lie, and I was nowhere near where I wanted to be, in life.

The question she posed to me was, "You do realize you can't make somebody happy if they're not happy with themselves, right?"

I was stunned! How could this be true? That was too easy of a revelation of the simple truth. How could I have not realized this before now? My mind and heart were racing as I tried to make peace with this bit of reality. What this meant to me was that I needed to face my situation without any excuses.

For the first time in my life, I was about to greet reality face-to-face. On that very day, I made up my mind that my life needed to change. I needed to take the steps toward making this change.

...talk about a sobering reality to deal with... I had to face someone who had been a major part of my life and tell her that my life was about to change – that *she* was a part of this change. At this point, I had to ignore everything but the facts and deal with the situation, or this change could never take place.

I sat down and defined my goals. I had to do some research and figure out what it was going to take to make them happen. A painful piece of the change meant getting a divorce and starting over. It meant maybe living apart from my sons. It meant going back to school for more education. It meant sacrificing my weekends in the name of making me a better person. *Was I really up for this challenge? Could I really pull this off? I must be crazy to think I could actually get where I wanted to be in life.*

The more I thought about the situation, the more it made sense to me. I had to do this to be a better person, to be a better father, and to achieve the rest of my goals. I can tell that you **the road was tough**, and it was an emotional journey I do not wish upon anyone – but it needed to happen. Your situation might not be as drastic as mine, but it will still take being honest with yourself and answering the question in this chapter's title (question) – without any reserve.

-Isaiah

Are you where you want to be?

NOTES:

8

From Hoping to Knowing

Part of being successful is believing in yourself. If you believe in yourself, then you'll be able to believe in other people. Most people truly believe that they'll finish what they start, otherwise they wouldn't start it. So then, why don't they finish it? Something happens; life happens; something doesn't come through on time; somebody forgets to do an important step; or they just get sidetracked by other things. Whatever the reason is, it's apparently enough to keep them from finishing what they started.

But, if they stop allowing themselves to be sabotaged by other people, other things, or themselves, then they'll see a way to push through that obstacle and finish well. That success will cause them to believe more strongly that they can accomplish something. Then, they will start something, work through issues that arise, and finish that task. Success leads to success and builds up the level of belief. The process repeats itself, but with a higher level of confidence.

With increased belief comes an improved vision. When you go **from *hoping*** that you'll finish something, **to *knowing*** that you'll finish it, your whole attitude changes! You no longer dread starting a new task…you actually look forward to it. Why? Because you now have the perspective and knowledge of how to work through bumps in the road that may have stopped you before.

With every new success comes an increase in experience, tenacity, and self-assuredness. All of those ingredients combine to improve your vision in life. You can almost anticipate how something is going to turn out, because you take control of your part, instead of letting it idly cruise along.

Move from hoping to knowing.

NOTES:

_____

_____

_____

_____

9

Miracles, Luck, and Strokes of Genius

Sometimes to achieve a dream, we need a break – some sort of miracle, luck, or stroke of genius. Thank goodness it appears when we need it the most. We may be in a really dark spot or just stuck in the same place for a while. Either way, we need something to break the friction that is keeping us from moving forward.

Miracles, luck, and strokes of genius are still alive and well in the world. People of all ages and of all walks of life continuously testify to the validity and reality of those three things. Tomorrow, while you're out and about during the day, pay attention to what people are saying, and see if you hear how many times people mention something that sounds like a miracle, luck, or stroke of genius. Then acknowledge it, and smile to yourself – you will have just witnessed greatness in the universe.

Right now, think of some time that one of those three things happened in your own life. When did some miraculous thing, bit of luck, or mind-bending answer show up and resolve an issue that you were facing? Did it happen today? Yesterday? A few years ago? When it did occur, did you give thanks for it? I hope so. If not, then it's not too late. You still can, right now.

Next, think about something that you're presently going through that makes you think you'll need another of the three to show up. Is it a big issue? Is it small? Does it involve other people? Whatever the situation is, the right sized answer will show up, just at the right time.

Greatness will still happen in your life, every day.

Expect it!

NOTES:

_____

_____

_____

_____

_____

BELIEVE. DO. AND FOLLOW THROUGH!

SECTION II:

DO.

10

Focus on Your End Goal

Sometimes, you have to start something by looking at the end of it in order to wind up where you want to go – because if you know where you want to go, you'll head in the right direction. Then, by keeping that route in focus, year after year, the way to get there will become clearer and easier.

> **When you are dropped into the moment,
> you are placed where you are meant to be.**

When things don't go the way you planned, ask yourself, "How in the world did I wind up in this spot? Did I come down this road on purpose, or did I just wind up here by default?"

> In general, how are you living...by design or by default? Purposed-living is the only way to go. All the rest is just bunk. Are you ready to move ahead, to leave your comfort zone, and to become the amazing creation you are destined to be? I hope so, because I'm ready for you to overcome and live out

loud, too. As you succeed in life, you remind others that living the status quo is not worth it.

To the right of my desk, on the wall in my office at home, I have a quote hanging. It's there as a constant reminder that there is a time to act, be decisive, and do something about the current situation – whatever that situation may be. Here's the quote that kicks me in the rear when I need it:

> There is a tide in the affairs of men
> Which, taken at the flood, leads on to fortune;
> Omitted, all the voyage of their life
> Is bound in shallows and in miseries.
> On such a full sea are we now afloat,
> And we must take the current when it serves,
> Or lose our ventures.
> "Julius Caesar" (Act IV, Scene iii)

If that doesn't speak "DO SOMETHING!" then I don't know what will. That quote has spurred me on to accomplish things and to keep going when I have wanted to quit, not finish writing a book, or do something else besides what I knew I needed to be doing.

It has also reminded me that success is possible, real, and ever-present in every endeavor we so choose to put our hands to. These are not light words that I am sharing. I know that they are true, because I have experienced them. They're real – that's for sure. Just as Shakespeare knew something profound about the human psyche and spirit hundreds of years ago, I know that those same principles and ideas hold true, today. I encourage you to go out and live them yourself, too! You can, <u>if you will</u>.

- *Marty*

Focus on your end goal.

NOTES:

_____

_____

_____

_____

_____

_____

_____

11

Break Big Things into Smaller Pieces

Hopefully by now, you've figured out what it is that you want to accomplish. Is it little? Is it big? Is it gigantic? No matter how big your dream may seem, it can be achieved, one step at a time:

1. First, list out all the steps involved in order of importance: most to least.
2. Then, start working on the most important thing.
3. Chip away at it, bit by bit, and eventually it will get done.
4. Repeat this process, over and over, until you work through all of the steps.
5. When you have a step that seems too big to handle, break it into smaller pieces.

Doing that will make the things doable. Making things into doable formats not only helps you succeed at doing whatever you're working on, it helps you have a better attitude about other things in your life.

It's like the proverbial question and answer, "How do you eat an elephant? One bite at a time." Some tasks really are big, while some just seem like it. Either way, if you break things into manageable chunks, the work is doable.

And... success breeds success. So, once you check one thing off your list, you'll feel better about getting the rest done.

As you work through each of the steps that you list out and become successful at them, you'll develop a system of accomplishment that works for you. That's when the rest of it will make sense – with each piece falling in line with the next.

If you try to do everything at once, you'll get overwhelmed and quit. But, if you do things bit-by-bit, then it's manageable – you'll be able to make it all the way through.

Remember, greatness doesn't happen overnight, and it doesn't happen all at once.

Greatness happens bit by bit.

12

Seeds of Greatness

Everyone has the ability to take what they have, who they are, and where they live – and turn it into something incredible. We each have seeds of greatness. It's how we utilize them that matters.

> I truly believe that the seeds of greatness are put inside of everyone when they are created. It wasn't like God forgot to put them in some people – He didn't. Everybody got 'em!
>
> So, why do some people act like they missed out? Maybe it's just that some people's seeds didn't get the right amount of nourishment when they were growing up, or maybe some people buried their seeds too deep! Either way, the seeds of greatness are still in there.
>
> Growing up on a dairy farm, I shoveled a lot of manure. I didn't know that God was just preparing me to work in public service for a couple of decades after that... What does that have to do with seeds of greatness? A lot.
>
> Since we had lots of fresh fertilizer, my dad taught my brother, sister, and me how to grow a garden

from scratch. He showed us how covering seeds with too much manure would burn up the seeds, and they wouldn't produce anything.

At the same time, he took some other seeds and planted them in a pot in the basement at home – showing us how important being out in the fresh air and sunlight were to those seeds – because they didn't grow very well in the dark.

Finally, he showed us how – with the right balance and amounts of all the different aspects of the environment – some of the seeds grew into healthy plants...meaning that when we treated the seeds the right way, they did what they knew to do – what they were meant to do.

There've been a number of times that I've looked at people at work and in my neighborhood and thought, "They're getting too much 'manure' put on them. They're gonna burn out!" or... "They're living in the dark. They either need to get brighter or get out more often!"

BUT, I keep telling myself that they still have seeds of greatness in them that need nourishment or that need to be re-discovered.

- Marty

You, too, have seeds of greatness in you! Help them grow! Help them flourish! And you'll be amazed at how awesome your life will become.

Today, before another minute of life passes, think about the seeds of greatness inside you. Are you using them to their fullest potential? Are they growing the way you want?

**Help them grow,
and you'll see
the difference in your life.**

NOTES:

_____

_____

_____

_____

_____

_____

_____

13

Just Do It

Everybody's familiar with the NIKE slogan "Just Do It"! Did NIKE get this right, or what?

First, they aimed their slogan at the shoes and clothes that people wear while they're playing their favorite sports. Then, NIKE surrounded itself with the world's best athletes in order to associate their name with the greatest success.

How could they go wrong?

If you think about the NIKE slogan, "Just Do It" and how it applies to your own life, it's the one thing that people need the most to get their lives going in the right direction.

How often do you tell yourself you're going to make a change in your life, but you never get started because you have no earthly idea how to get started on making that change? The best way to initiate change is to just do it!

Don't let your mind go into excuse mode or say, *"I'm going to do it...after I do [this or that]."* That's one of the most common things you'll hear people say about losing weight, too. People who are planning to lose weight have long lists of things they are going to do...*once they lose* those 5, 10 or 20-pounds. If you have lists of excuses, stop letting that be your crutch for not getting your life moving in the direction you want it to go.

> After I remarried, my wife and I developed a great motivational tool that we've used to keep our focus, on a yearly basis. We both write down five things we want to do in the coming year. We post this on the back of our bathroom door. You wouldn't believe how this has motivated us.
>
> In the first year of trying it, we completed 8 of the 10 things on the list!
>
> How did we succeed? We held each other accountable for the list we made, and we served as a support system for each other. Those two simple methods yielded fantastic results kept us focused on our goals.
>
> I encourage you to try this method to get your life moving in the direction you want it to go.
>
> *--Isaiah*

Do it!

14

Doing, with Purpose

When people do things to simply justify their own existence, they have lost sight of their reasons for being here. Living each day is more than just checking off your TO DO list, eating, and sleeping. There are deeper meanings to the whole series of actions that occur physically and spiritually.

> Over the years at work, I've sometimes lost sight of my greater purpose in teaching, mentoring, etc. My wife, Kristine, has always encouraged me to not give up on students, colleagues, or situations.
>
> Sometimes, it takes more convincing than others, but in the end, she always helps me to remember that the work I do each day doesn't really matter – what matters is the lives of the people that I come in contact with...they matter.
>
> That reminder helps me re-center, mentally and spiritually. It helps to be reminded that when I "do" the work I do, it's with a greater purpose. Thanks, Kristine!
>
> *- Marty*

Physiologically, connections are made between action and purpose. The end results are lived-out activity, emotional connection, synapse creation, and creation of memory. If you only look at the initial action, you're missing the bigger picture. If you remember the bigger picture – what your end result is – then, while you're in the middle of the mundane actions, you'll be able to maintain energy to finish the job. May heaven help those who lose sight of the bigger picture.

Keep the bigger picture in mind.

NOTES:

_____

_____

_____

_____

_____

_____

_____

15

Living with Perceptions

Perceptions have become the ruling factor in everything we see or believe. Perceptions set the standards by which others judge us. Most people don't realize the power perceptions have in the business world, as well as in daily interactions in our communities.

> Often, we find that perceptions can be false, but it still doesn't excuse the fact that they have a major influence on our success.
>
> One situation that comes to mind, was going to a car dealership and trying to get assistance. My wife and I had just come from the water slide, so our attire was very casual. We stopped at a local dealership to look at a new truck, for *me*. I had my eye on a new Ford F-150 Supercrew.
>
> Well, as life goes, we walked around the dealership for about 20 minutes before anyone approached us or even asked if we needed any assistance. Once the first contact was made, the salesman began showing us everything *except* what I went there to look at.

Finally, I told him I wanted to look at a new F-150 Supercrew, and his response was, "Those are pretty pricey vehicles."

I replied, "Really? How pricey are they?"

We slowly made our way over to three rows of trucks, as if we were wasting his time. We test drove an XLT version with cloth interior, and my wife said, "No way."

I then asked him for a Lariat – with all the bells and whistles. He looked at me in amazement, like, *"What does this guy know about our top-of-the-line truck?"*

He was reluctant to pull one out for a test drive. We finally got to drive one, though, and my wife and I knew that was what we wanted. Well, the color we wanted was three rows in, so *more* drama started.

The salesman asked if we were "serious about purchasing a truck," because it would be a large task to move the two rows of trucks to get to the one we wanted. I looked him sternly in the eye and said, "If you want to sell a truck tonight, you better start moving trucks."

The drama didn't stop there... We went inside to do the paperwork, and they pulled our credit – their attitudes changed 180 degrees! All of sudden, I became *"Mr. Whittaker"*....and the salesman quickly asked, "Would you like something to drink?"

There still was one big problem. That dumb guy was catering to *me*, instead of to *my wife*, and that was when his night became very hard!

I was filling out paperwork, when my wife asked to "assist" me...the rest was history. She took control of the situation and informed the salesman that *she* would be purchasing the truck *on her own*, because she had a job *and* the credit score to do it.

I just shrugged my shoulders and said, "Talk to *her*." The end result was – I was getting my truck.

Well, the contract came out from the finance office, and it was off by sixty cents a month. My wife demanded they do the contract, again. The finance guy lost his mind, but regained it when he realized she wasn't joking.

She even made them fill the truck up with gas, before we drove off, waving a sarcastic "Thanks, guys!"

--Isaiah

Perceptions controlled this whole transaction – without a doubt – at several junctions. Think about this the next time perceptions become *your* main focus.

Be careful of perceptions.

BELIEVE. DO. AND FOLLOW THROUGH!

NOTES:

16

Do Something – Don't Just "Plan"

Lack of action is one of the greatest killers of success. Some people are great planners, but they rarely follow through on what they "planned to do." Sound familiar? How many lists of "things to do" do you have lying around your house? Right now, go and get one of them.

Have it in hand? Okay, pick something on the list, and go do it. When you're done, come back to this page…

Did you do something on the list? If so, great! Cross it out. According to the 80/20 rule, you just proved that you're part of the 20 percent of society who does 80 percent of the work, because you actually DID something.

Planning and planning and talking about doing something – without ever actually doing it – is enough to drive you batty. A couple of my dear friends suffer from this condition. They have great ideas, make detailed lists of things they're "gonna" do, but never DO anything with them.

To me, that's like planning a fun road trip without ever executing the plan. How frustrating would that be?! For example, if I'm going to drive from Charlotte to Atlanta, I don't stay in my driveway, looking under the hood. No!

Sure, I check the fluids, the tires, and everything else. THEN, (here's the key) I get in the car and DRIVE. As long as I keep going, later that day I'll be in Atlanta. In order to get to my destination, I have to stop planning and start driving.

The same thing holds true for life.

Do something.

NOTES:

_____

_____

_____

_____

_____

17

Why? Because Your Life Counts!

Why do we keep encouraging you to BELIEVE in yourself, to BELIEVE in others, and to DO positive things? ...Because your life counts. You count! So many times, people act as if what they do doesn't matter, but it does! It really does.

When you wake up in the morning, the day is fresh, you're renewed, and you have a new start of making everything happen that you want. Ultimately, the only deadline that you have is the one of your life ending. Otherwise, every other deadline that you face is self-imposed or someone else-imposed. When you realize that, then you'll have a whole new perspective about what you do and how you do it.

People often ask, "If you knew that you could not fail, what would you attempt?" If they truly believed that idea, they ought to ask, "If you knew that you could not fail, what would you *complete*?" You may think, "That's just semantics...the difference of only one word..." True, and one word, in this sense, is just like the difference of one degree when it comes to boiling water. Water at 211°

Fahrenheit, you have really hot water, but at 212°F, you can move ships around the world! The difference is only one degree, one word, one idea - but it makes *all* the difference in the world.

When time seems to stop for you on a daily basis (time doesn't really stop…it's a mental thing…), what do you do with those moments? Do you maximize them? Do you enjoy them? Do you even realize that they are occurring? Most of the time, people don't even realize that it's happening; they just joyfully, or blindly, go traipsing through the day without realizing that the universe has opened itself up to them and is giving them a glimpse of what *could* be possible.

So, the next time that the world "stops" for a moment, take that opportunity to "get off the merry-go-round" and reflect on what it is that you're supposed to realize. There's a special moment in your day that determines what the rest of the day is going to be like. When you see that there is greatness in the midst of that moment, you'll start maximizing those opportunities that briefly appear. Stop letting them get away! Grab onto them! They were meant for you!

Your life counts!

18

Enjoy What You Do

In the midst of working towards your goals and achieving your dreams, it's important to enjoy what you do. Because, if you don't enjoy it, what's the point of even doing it, really? Sure, we all want to get things done and check them off our lists, but if we approach work from the attitude of rote action, we're no good to anyone. Life is too short to simply go through it on "autopilot."

Besides, there are already plenty of people who do jobs and work at things that they don't enjoy. So, break the mold! Do something you enjoy, and enjoy what you do!

> One morning at "first breakfast" (*before* going to milk the cows), my dad allowed me to see into his life a little more. We were talking about careers, work, etc.
>
> Midway through starting to take a sip of coffee, he set his cup down on the table and semi-stared off into space. Then, he looked at me and said, "Do something you like, and you won't wake up every day feeling like you're running into a brick wall, head first, for forty years."

Ironically, when I've run that idea by different people, I've gotten lots of different responses:

- "If I did what I love to do, I'd be broke."

- "If you do what you love to do, then it'll become work, and you won't love it, anymore."

- "Hobbies are for what you love to do. Work is called 'work,' because that's what it is."

- "If I did my hobby as work, then what would I have to look forward to on the weekends?"

    ...and finally...

- "Absolutely! I've done what I love to do for thirty years – and still love it!"

For a while, I thought that if I could match up people I asked with occupations that they didn't like, then I would figure out a magic formula. It finally dawned on me that it still goes back to individuals and their personal likes and dislikes – how they were made – and what they were created to do. I started looking for the gleam in people's eyes or the lack thereof.

Years later, I came across the book, *Do What You Love, The Money Will Follow*. As I flipped through the pages, my dad's comment to me at "o'dark-thirty," years before, came running back to the front of my mind, "Do something you like, and you won't wake up every day feeling like you're running into a brick wall, head first, for forty years."

--Marty

Enjoy what you do!

NOTES:

_____

_____

_____

_____

_____

_____

_____

_____

19

Living Through Expectations!

So often we get so caught up in living up to expectations that others set for us. We get so accustomed to this type of living that we eventually lose touch with reality. This is "living the BIG lie" – not being in touch with yourself and being dishonest to your own beliefs.

There are people reading these words, right now, that have lost their grasp on reality and just need to look within to break this vicious cycle.

A WARNING to those who break the cycle:
…You might find yourself alone drinking a cup of coffee, instead of with the normal morning gathering of fans…

The best part about this, though, is you get the opportunity to regain yourself. Everyone – at some point in life – has lost touch with reality. This is not hard to do, because we all want to be accepted by our peers or to obtain some certain social status.

One of my personal challenges in living through expectations was trying to live up to the standards my parents set for my sister and me. Getting a college education was **not** optional. I felt this was something I had to achieve, just to exist in this world we live in. That was a lot of pressure I carried around with me, because I had no idea what I wanted to do in this giant world that we are all supposed to go out into and just start living in. I think early on I lacked discipline and dedication to committing to selecting a career or pursuing a degree in a certain discipline.

Now, I look back and I realize I made a choice to live up to those expectations. Not once did I ask **why** getting a college education was so important in my parents' eyes. The examples they set for me seemed very normal, and I thought that they were the same expectations everybody else my age was living with.

- Isaiah

Are you living up to expectations set by some outside force? Have you lost touch with your own personal reality? Stop – and take time to evaluate how you are truly living. Stop letting others determine what your expectations in life should be. Get in touch with your own reality.

**Live through expectations,
and keep on living!**

NOTES:

Section III:

And Follow Through!

20

Live Out Your Purpose in Life

There's an excitement in the air when you start living the life that you were meant to live. People around you will sense it, and hopefully it will inspire them to realize that their lives count, too. But even if some of them don't, *you* still have the obligation to the universe and to humanity to fulfill your purpose in life and to achieve your full potential.

Once you see that, you can't walk away. You have to live out that purpose, no matter what. Oh, you can try to walk away from it, but it'll tear you up inside. If you try to run away from the words that go through your head every day, it will be hell on earth. But, when you submit to the greater purposes in your life, then all will be well.

It may seem that some things aren't working out the way you want them to. If that's the case, it's usually because you don't see the things that are happening "behind the scenes."

Take gardeners, for example: when they plant seeds, they typically put them in rows or in some part of their yard, on purpose. Then at the appointed time, the seeds break forth into song and pop up out of the ground as beautiful flowers or vegetables. However, a few of the seeds don't come up. It's as if they disappear from the face of the earth, but in reality, they don't. Birds eat some of them; a few get choked out by weeds; and others get put in bad soil, by mistake, and die.

Although you might be in bad soil right now, you are not a mistake. You were not born by accident. You are here for a reason. When you realize that wonderful truth, you will begin to do amazing things. You are valuable, important, and incredible. Allow God to work in your life, and He will show you how to unleash the greatness that He put inside you when He knit you together.

When we waltz into the days of life that allow us to easily do what we are meant to do, we are operating in the God-given talents and abilities that we are strongest in. No matter what the world says, when we are where we are supposed to be, there is no denying that we are definitely driven by the right forces.

Time will show that determination pays off. It gets stronger with time, allowing us to see deeper into the realms of life – moments ticking away on the clock and counting for something greater than ourselves.

Here are some questions to keep in mind, as you progress in your successes:

- What is your life's work?
- What are you dedicated to?
- What are you committed to?
- What are you willing to do, no matter what?
- What are you *not* willing to do, no matter what?
- What are you most excited about during the day?
    - Being here?
    - Going there?
- Working in this realm?
- Standing where no one will see you?
- Standing in the spotlight?
- What are your immovable core values and beliefs?

How you answer each of those will determine where you invest your life's energy.

Live out your purpose!

BELIEVE. DO. AND FOLLOW THROUGH!

NOTES:

21

How to Handle Distractions

Handling distractions when you're trying to focus on a goal or when you're making a positive change in your life can be a challenge, especially if you are easily sidetracked.

Self-Inventory
We've found that the best approach to handling distractions is to face them head-on – by doing what we call "self-inventory." Self-inventory starts with assessing the situation and follows with asking yourself a series of questions.

Identify the Distraction
The first thing to do is <u>honestly identify the distraction</u>: Is it a thing? A hobby? A television show? A person? The Internet? A bad habit? An addiction? Gossip?

Place a Value
Next, place a value on the distraction and the effect it is having on you or your situation. Is it important to you?

If so, how important? How much is the distraction worth (time-wise, financially, emotionally, etc)?

3 Big Questions
Then, ask yourself three big questions:

1. Can this distraction help me reach my goal faster?

2. Will this distraction keep me from reaching my goal *within the milestones* I set when I planned my goals?

…and the biggest question…
3. Will this distraction *ultimately keep me from* reaching my goal?

The answers you discover will reveal a lot. When you answer all your questions, you should a have a pretty good idea of what to do about the distraction.

Types
There are all types of distractions: things, people, worries, good intentions, regrets, anger, or even the pursuit of perfection. Two of the biggest ones can be material things and family issues.

Material Things
You can have fun with some really cool stuff in life, but when you use them to hide behind, you're no longer pursuing your goals – you're wasting time.

Unless the gadgets and doodads you're messing with are directly helping you achieve your goals, they're distractions and time-stealers.

Somebody once said that the more stuff you have, the more time and money it takes to maintain it. Some people even try to fill voids in their lives with material things, instead of developing healthy relationships.

Family Issues
Family issues can be a distraction. We're not saying you need to ignore your family to reach your goals – far from it! But you have to find a balance and decide how your family situation is going to impact you in reaching your goals.

This is a very tough topic to address, but so many people hide behind family obligations as a reason for not reaching their goals. To reach your goals or make positive changes in your life, you have to find a balance that addresses your family needs and concerns, while pursuing goals that they will also benefit from.

Distractions are always going to come and go. The key is how you handle them. Are you going to let them turn into excuses? Will you be honest with your self-inventory and deal with the distractions appropriately?

As a Test
Distractions can also be used in a positive manner to test your plans for achieving your goals. People may simply be trying to see how serious you are about reaching your goals. If you bragged about goals in the past but did little to achieve them, then your spouse, kids, friends, or co-workers may be trying to see if you really are going to "rock the world" this time. Inside, they truly do want you to succeed, because every time you do, you raise the level of life around you.

Lastly, no plan ever makes it through without getting modified in some way. That's just the nature of the beast when it comes to reaching goals and making positive changes in your life. So, what to do? Let it be modified; be flexible; and keep going!

Face distractions head-on!

22

Tenacity

Tenacity is stubbornness with a purpose. In order to achieve different things, you need to have a certain amount of tenacity. Most things aren't going to be given to you, so you'll have to work at them until you succeed. Giving up along the way may seem like an option, but don't take it. Leave that for the people who are happy with the status quo.

When you're tenacious, you'll go the extra mile, do the extra part, or stand a little longer than other people will. How badly you want something will add to your tenacity. There's not a magic formula for making yourself more tenacious, but tenacity does "kick in" when you need it. It's almost like a switch flips in your head – stubbornness makes you dig your heels into the ground, and the reason you're fighting so hard keeps you focused on achieving your goal. It just happens. It's almost as if the primal part of your human spirit rises up out of the modern, technological fluff and overcomes all circumstances to win.

Nurses and doctors see it all the time with patients in hospitals who have a reason to live: they can literally be "on their deathbed" one day and be completely turned around the next. The will to live kicks in and spurs on the rest of the body. The body starts to fight and wins.

Patients who aren't ready to die, yet, have the tenacity to overcome their situations and strike back at death's calling. They've harbored energy and have summoned strength from deep places. They bring that fight to the surface and command their bodies to live.

The spirit is greater than the flesh, by far. We command our bodies to be subject to the demands of the mind and can overcome all obstacles.

Live out the tenacity that's already in you. Let your spirit shine forth into the world and into the lives of others.

Be tenacious!

23

Choose to Live Differently

Do words cause us to act, or is it the nuances that surround them? Do they develop from nothingness, on their own, or are they caused in our minds by the greatness of the Universe and its purposes? We are trapped in between the greatness that exists and the mediocrity that tries so strongly to drag us down with it.

We can step above those surroundings and draw unto the purposes that wait for us to awaken and realize their existence. By our words, we propose we are aware of supreme ideas that control the Universe, but our actions sometimes reveal otherwise. We squabble for bits of faded glory, when we could be reaching and living toward the wholeness and grandeur that awaits.

If we would simply look beyond the immediate – beyond the tangible – we would lay hold of intangible, yet meaningful parts of life, construct them, and make them tangible. It is possible to live in that manner, yet so few choose to do so. Those who choose to live differently – to go down that path of overcoming – will not have many companions during the venture. Yet, those who are on the same path are also of the same character and stature. So, if you go, you will find good company.

Carefully consider the options, and then purposefully choose which way you want to live. However, if you continue to hesitate and refuse to choose, you will still have chosen. Avoidance doesn't negate the existence of the option – it only dictates a singular route that you may dislike.

Follow through on what you start. Finish well. A lot of people start things that they don't finish. Not finishing things can lead to a frustrating set of days, which could turn into a frustrating life. We've all seen people who just seem to be grumpy all the time. Don't be like them. Follow through on what you start. In the days that stretch out before you, you will find the purpose you were meant to live, if you don't already know what it is.

Live differently.

24

Lean into the Wind

Sometimes, you have to just turn around and face the storm; lean into the wind; and push forward. Drops of rain might sting your face; flurries of life might blind you. YET, while the world around you shouts that you can't make it, if you lean into wind, you will.

Stamina gets developed when we stand firm and continue to fight for what we know is right. One of the ways to find peace in our lives is to do what we know is correct, work hard, and enjoy rest. We all get tired and grow weary. When that happens, rest - whether it's for a few minutes, a few hours, or longer ...rest. It'll rejuvenate your body, your mind, and your spirit – all of which will give you a renewed perspective on your job, project, or life. You'll come back full of spunk and fire. The gleam will return to your eyes, and you'll be able to handle most of the things that life throws at you.

One of the fastest ways to raise your spirit is to listen to your favorite music. It brings up positive memories and replaces dreadful images with things that put a smile on your face. It's not possible for your heart to be full of joy and not have a smile on your face to match. One automatically happens with the other – sort of like pedaling a tandem bike.

We are all able – because we were made so.

> "It doesn't matter what you've heard –
> 'Impossible' is not a word –
> It's just a reason for someone not to try."
>
> *--Kutless*

Lean in.

NOTES:

_____

_____

_____

_____

_____

25

Overcome

The times that life slaps us in the face are times in which we have to stand our ground and fight back. Nothing will be given to you for free in this life beyond love, grace, and beauty. People respect you for who you are and for standing firm in your beliefs. Don't be wishy-washy – it doesn't serve well. Belittling other people will tear you down – not that it will kill you, but it will keep you from moving forward. It'll hold you back on the inside, because you'll know you're guilty. Speak the truth in love, but don't run away from love – it only pushes your true emotions further down than they should go.

What's holding you back in life? Thoughts? Ideas? Other people? You? Move forward. Attack the issues that you're dealing with. Make them small enough to consume them, and finish them off. Don't let them rule your world. Make them become subject to your will and not the other way around.

You have dominion over your fears and your shortcomings. When God made you, He didn't make you in an image of timidity and limp living!

He made you in His image – in the image of the Almighty Creator of the universe. Man, that's powerful! Start living like that.

Don't let the world dictate your actions and life any more. Dictate to the world that you're going to overcome and are going to live in positive, powerful ways, every day, from now until the end of your life. If you'll do that, you'll truly be amazed in a very short time just how powerfully good the effects of your life are. You are free to choose success, to live it every day, and to become the person you were meant to be! Go for it!

To overcome something means to figure out a way to go around it, under it, over it, or through it. Whichever way you choose to do it, it must be done, if you're going to overcome. There's no other way.

Have you ever seen plants that grow up through cracks in a sidewalk or on the steep side of rock face cliff? Those plants are simply doing what they were designed to do – they grow – no matter where – no matter what. They grow. The harsh surroundings make them tough. If those plants can overcome "their situations in life," think about how much more you can.

Part of living successfully is consistently doing the hard things that other people are not willing to do. Why? Because that's one of the things that separates you from the rest. By doing what other people aren't willing to do, you prove that you have the moxie to get it done. Then, by consistently doing those things – day in, day out – you prove to yourself that you really are different than a lot of other people. Is it easy? No. Is it worth it? Definitely.

What it comes down to is this:
Is what you're trying to accomplish worth the pain associated with the effort it will take to overcome the obstacles in your way?

>...If your answer is "No," then stop doing that, and do something else.

>...If your answer is "Yes," then press on, and don't quit until you've broken through the frustrations and have safely reached the other side.

If you choose to press on, will you come through on the other side tarnished and burnt? Maybe. Is it worth it? Yes, if that's what it takes to achieve your dream.

How much you do depends on how badly you want it. Do you want it badly enough? Do you? If so, then do what it takes to reach the other side of overcoming. Don't stop until you've broken through and have accomplished all that you set out to do. You can do it. No doubt about it.

Flip the mental switch in your head, and figure out a way to succeed. The human spirit is stronger than most people give it credit.

You are an amazing creation. Live like it.

You have it in you to succeed. Just do it.

There was nothing lacking in your initial make-up as a person, when you came into the world. Think back to the earliest points in your life, and realize just how many things from then 'til now that you have lived through and have survived…think of all the times you've won and overcome…you are a capable human being – live like it.

Overcome.

26

Realization of a Dream

Oftentimes, what appears to be ingenious or an "overnight success" is actually something that took years of work, retries, successes, and failures. Likewise, someone will do things that seem odd, stupid, SciFi-ish, or just plain weird. Then years later, other people will exclaim how brilliant and "ahead of his time" he was!

Ironic, isn't it?

All of those ideas bring to mind the fantastic movie, *Bottle Shock*. Based on a true story, it tells about the interconnected lives of half a dozen people, all trying to achieve their different dreams.

One of the main characters, Jim Barrett (the dad), had given up his partnership in a successful law firm in order to pursue his dream of making the world's best wine. Tirelessly working year after year, he experienced a number of successes and failures. In the process, he had become an expert in winemaking, but few people outside of his immediate community knew it. His pride, stubbornness, and self-perception were part of the problem.

Finally, he hit rock bottom: he was out of money and his latest effort had failed – the Chardonnay they spent so much time perfecting turned out murky-brown, instead of staying clear.

He was done.

He called some guys to come haul away the 500 cases of bad wine, and with his old, leather briefcase in hand, he drove to his old law firm.

He had worked so hard and had tried so many times to succeed. Having to go back to where he had left must have been the ultimate sense of failure for him.

BUT...

While he was in a pit of despair, other people and other forces were working in his favor. As fate would have it, the Chardonnay went back to being clear. It turned out to be perfect – absolutely delicious and beautifully colored!

As Jim Barrett was in the midst of giving up, all of the pieces came together and produced for him the realization of his dream.

Later, at a "blind taste" wine competition in Paris, judges declared Barrett's Chardonnay to be Number 1 in the world.

He had done it. He HAD produced the perfect Chardonnay – the best in the world. He realized his dream.

At the time, some of Barrett's friends and colleagues told him that he was foolish for attempting what he did. Yet, decades later, the world still acclaims his achievement and continuing successes.

Ironic, isn't it?

**What dreams
are you trying to achieve or realize?**

What things are you about to give up on?

Don't quit. While you have been toiling away, other people and other forces have been at work in your favor. You just haven't seen them. That's the way it works, sometimes.

Just when you are about to give up hope, your greatest success can still occur. Your greatest miracle can yet show up.

See it through, and you will be amazed! You, too, will then be able to say that you have been blessed with the Realization of a Dream.

Realize your dream!

NOTES:

_____

_____

_____

_____

_____

_____

_____

_____

_____

27

Handling Success and Recognition

How you handle the fame you receive will show the character that was developed in you during the fameless, struggling times. Whatever character that was built in you before this current moment, is the character that will show forth if stardom ever hits. Meanwhile, all of the people that you interact with on a daily basis will benefit, or not, from your currently-existing character.

Does this make sense?

Think about it: All of the people that you come into contact with each day: how do they perceive you to be in real life? Whether that's how you mean to be or not, that's how you "come across."

Perceptions are interesting things…that's not to say go out and live solely how you want others to think of you. Instead, consciously be aware of your subconscious actions.

Because in the end, you're going to live the way you want to, anyway…This is an encouragement for you to do it consciously and with gusto.

Handle success graciously!

NOTES:

___

___

___

___

___

___

___

___

28

Savor Life, One Moment at a Time

Some people try to find happiness and fulfillment in jobs, experiences, or other people, instead of by simply living their lives, everyday. Happiness and fulfillment are real and can be enjoyed, if people will let things happen that were meant to happen. When they try to force things to happen, they cause roadblocks in their minds and obstacles in their lives. They have to realize that all of life doesn't happen at once – it's a process – a lifetime. We forget that, sometimes, and get all bent out of shape, because things aren't happening as fast as we think they should.

When you sit down to eat dinner, do you open your mouth and shove all your food in at the same time? Of course not! You would never do that. You can't fit the entire plate of food in there at once, let alone enjoy it. Life is the same way – why would you expect to be able to do everything, let alone enjoy it, all at the same time?

BELIEVE. DO. AND FOLLOW THROUGH!

**Just as you savor a meal
one bite at a time,
savor life
one moment at a time.**

My Goals
(1 week, 1 month, 1 year, 5 years, etc.)

_____

_____

_____

_____

_____

_____

_____

_____

_____

_____

_____

_____

_____

_____

BELIEVE. DO. AND FOLLOW THROUGH!

*What I BELIEVE about myself
in relation to my goals:*

_____

_____

_____

_____

_____

_____

_____

_____

_____

_____

_____

_____

_____

What I need to DO to make my goals a reality:

_____

_____

_____

_____

_____

_____

_____

_____

_____

_____

_____

_____

_____

BELIEVE. DO. AND FOLLOW THROUGH!

What I need to FOLLOW THROUGH on to make my goals a reality:

_____

_____

_____

_____

_____

_____

_____

_____

_____

_____

_____

_____

_____

_____

Epilogue

We hope that you've learned a lot about yourself by reading this book. We've enjoyed sharing our ideas, experiences, and stories with you! We also hope that our attempts, failures, and successes in life will encourage you to keep smiling and moving forward.

If you always live purposefully, you'll see sunshine in the end!

We look forward to meeting you in the pages of another one of our books or at a presentation.

Remember,

Believe.
Do.
and Follow Through!

- Marty & Isaiah